Lorette Pruden has managed to pack years of business experience and lessons learned into one easy-to-read, invaluable book, which will revolutionize your business strategy. Formerly Corporate gets straight to the heart of how past corporate employees turned independent business owners can transform their corporate mindset and restructure their network to systematically build a thriving 21st century business. Whether you are just starting out in business, trying to get unstuck, or ardently staying the course, I highly recommend you save yourself the trouble of braving the pitfalls of business on your own and, instead, allow this book to be your go-to guide.

Ivan Misner, Ph.D.,
NY Times Bestselling Author & Founder of BNI®

Lorette Pruden's new book, Formerly Corporate: Mindset Shifts for Successes in Your Own Business will resonate with you (is a MUST read) whether you are just starting out in your first non-corporate adventure or you are already a "Conquering Entrepreneur." The gut punching questions and lessons must have been hard earned to enable her to offer the reader the insights and truths she so clearly provides!

Whether you are "hearing" for the first time, or just now realizing an entrepreneur's primary mantra, you must embrace the reality that you must "know what you don't know" and "find somebody that does", if you are to succeed as an entrepreneur.

William Brown
SVP - USA Practice Leader
International Center for Executive Options
Lee Hecht Harrison

If you don't know what the Entrepreneurial Mindset feels like or sounds like, read Pruden's book. It will help you screen-in how folks get paid, and separate in your own network the entrepreneur with a business plan from the job seeker with only a resume.

Whether you start a venture or want to back an entrepreneur you trust, you'll start by generating your own paycheck and create options through which to flourish. Before hitting the Venture Capital circuit, invest in this book to nurture your own right mindset for success and cultivate like-minded others.

Dan Conley,
OnCallCFO for Fundable Teams,
VenturEvaluator for the Angels & LifeInfoSci
Investors Network, NJAngels.net
Lead Advisor for Entrepreneurs University
programs

After 25 years as a business journalist, writing about why "formerly corporate" entrepreneurs succeed or fail, I read this book with delight. Pruden dispenses pungent warnings (business owners can often "smell the formerly corporate a mile away" and "Blunt advice here. You have to sell something." She has savvy suggestions for ways to meet potential clients, and to consult without "giving away the store." Pruden helps would-be business owners clarify their goals, clearly explains the standard solutions, and adds her own out-of-the-box ideas.

Barbara Figge Fox
Journalist & blogger at
www.princetoncomment.blogspot.com

FORMERLY CORPORATE

Mindset Shifts for Success in Your Own Business

By Lorette Pruden, PhD

Open Door Publications, LLC

FORMERLY CORPORATE™
Mindset Shifts for Success in Your Own Business

Copyright © 2013 by Lorette Pruden, PhD

ISBN: 978-0-9888319-3-3

Published by
Open Door Publications
2113 Stackhouse Dr.
Yardley, PA 19067
www.OpenDoorPublications.com

ACKNOWLEDGEMENTS

In acknowledging those who kick-started, influenced, assessed, enhanced and ultimately got me to finish this book, I have cast my thoughts over the last 13 years and found way too many people to name here. So as you'll expect, I name a few, omit the many, and thank them all.

First, my friend and business strategist, Kim Rowe. We are both independent consultants, and we built a small local business together. Now we meet on the beach a couple of times a year and plot our main business strategies. It works.

Next, my clients and associates whose stories I've told in this book: Charles Brumlik, Kolbe Clark and Kelley Evens, and Karen Miller.

Many others, especially Ed Keenan, Cheryl Sheasby, Noelle Stary, Amara Willey and Carl Muehleisen, who formed the core of ongoing peer advisory groups that were really the lab for the Starburst Business™ concept.

My whole cohort of Formerly Corporate™ clients, from start-ups to successful businesses, who have shown the courage and perseverance it takes to get here from there.

My professional colleagues, especially Art Radtke and Bill Davis of the Team Nimbus collective. Also, the members of my chapters in the National Speakers Association, the Institute for Management Consultants and Princeton Independent Consultants. And Dan Conley and our Entrepreneurs University colleagues who provide the window into the tech start-up world and angel investing.

In true Starburst fashion, Karen Hodges Miller has been editor, publisher, client and friend.

Vickie Sullivan of SullivanSpeakers.com and the National Speakers Association who kick-started (and re-kicked on occasion) me into telling the world what I had learned in the transformation from Formerly Corporate™ to what's happening now.

My brother, who knows a lot more than I do about a lot of things I need to know. And Todd and Sebastian and Grace, who make it all worthwhile.

It ain't over yet.

TABLE OF CONTENTS

The spotlight won't shine on you without effort. Don't listen only to yourself. Don't listen only to people too much like you. "I had those go-to people...!" You have more leverage and power than you think. Patience is a virtue.

Section Three:
The Conquering Hero Stumbles
Focus. Accountability. Urgency.
Focus. Accountability. Now.

Section Four:
Solutions: All Hail the Conquering Hero
The three characteristics.

How to recognize yourself as a Conquering Entrepreneur. Invent your own strategy. Your own Plan C. Information, introspection, into action.

SECTION ONE
What Happened?

The working world will never be the same

INTRODUCTION

The beginning of the 21st century has brought enormous change to the corporate landscape. Many of the great corporations of the last century have merged beyond recognition or are flat-out gone. And so are millions of corporate jobs. For example, in the mid-1980s, before the downsizing tsunami hit, both Exxon and Mobil had more than 180,000 employees each. They were the Number One and Number Two oil companies in the world when they merged in 1998 to become ExxonMobil, with a pre-merger total of 122,700 employees. Two years later, the number was down to 99,600, and the 2011 Annual Report of ExxonMobil reports 82,100 employees, less than a quarter of the total number of employees they had had in the 1980s.

The oil industry is just one example of how corporations are hiring fewer employees today. High tech industries are the oil companies of the 21st century, and they typically have thousands fewer employees than the traditional businesses of the mid- and late 20th century. Google, for example, had a little more than 30,000 employees in the third quarter of 2011. The net jobs lost since the Great Recession began in 2007 exceeds 8.8 million.[1] The percentage of the population employed dropped like a drone hit it. "In the four years following June 2007, the volume of business loans under $1 million fell 13%."[2]

But the people haven't gone. Where are they?

Right next door perhaps, or at the holiday dinner or unloading their kid's dorm stuff in the line right behind you. They may be at the gym, if they can still afford it or are still in denial that they can't, or walking in the neighborhood if they are more frugal or realistic.

We expect the unemployed or underemployed to look different—but they do not. In the suburbs and the exurbs the unemployed and the underemployed look just the same as you and me. Ordinary people, many well-educated and highly trained, hard and earnest workers, who had "good jobs" a few years ago, are the new unemployed. They are:

- The commercial loan banker with no loans to make.
- The creative director of a regional public broadcasting station that needed "fewer creatives."
- The global outsourcing director who has

---

[1] http://en.wikipedia.org/wiki/File:US_employment_1995-2012.png
[2] http://www.forbes.com/sites/joelkotkin/2013/03/13/wall-streets-hollow-boom-with-small-business-and-startups-lagging-employment-wont-pick-up/

been deemed redundant.

This book is not generation specific—the stories come from Baby Boomers, Gen X and Gen Y business owners. If you worked in a corporate job, or for someone else, before you started your own business, if you don't see W-2 jobs in your future—and you want your business to thrive, read on.

Since I am a boomer, though, I'll start with that story. In the 1970s, '80s and '90s, they worked Plan A —went to college, maybe got advanced degrees, went to work, did well, got promoted. They got married, had two kids, bought cars and houses. A lot of social changes swept them along, but they were living the American Dream. They worked for wages—W-2 wages. But that career—and that dream—and that way of getting paid ended. The company downsized, was bought, just plain folded. "We're sorry—it's not you. We just don't need so many people anymore," was what they heard—often two, three or more times. The retirement age increased to 66, then 67...but there were no jobs to retire from, and who could afford to retire, anyway?

What are they doing now? Many of them tried Plan B—they became small business owners or independent contractors. They got paid on the sales they made: in cash, or credit cards or as 1099s. Or not at all.

Byron Vielehr, president of global risk and analytics at D&B, wrote: "...2009 and 2010 bore witness to the highest percentage of startups in more than a decade. The rate of new businesses had also been steadily climbing since 2006. As a result, the number of businesses in 2010 compared to 2007 is higher." Even though, as he also says, the rate of business failures almost doubled between 2007 and 2009.[3]

Who started those businesses? Many eager or reluctant entrepreneurs are Formerly Corporate™ employees who took the severance package and the home equity loan and maybe drained the 401(k) to start a business. Building on their knowledge and experience, their drive and work ethic, their desire to stay rooted in the community they had lived in for years, they started service businesses, bought franchises, created alternative health practices, went into cooking or gardening or music as revenue-generating activities rather than hobbies.

I've said somewhat jokingly for years now, "Scratch any new (or five-year-old) small business owner in our New Jersey area and you'll find a Formerly Corporate™ chemical engineer, telecom worker, IT professional, administrative assistant, or other corporate worker." Then it was insurance and pharmaceutical and financial industry ejects. Now they have been joined by bankers, investment brokers and other employees from industries that were once considered "safe."

It doesn't matter what profession these Formerly Corporate™ employees came from. The jobs may change according to where they live, but the phenomenon is the same. If there's no job available, the enterprising person makes one!

For some, the transition has gone smoothly. They

---

[3] http://upstart.bizjournals.com/resources/social-media/2011/05/20/number-of-small-businesses-rose-since-recession.html?page=all

had a family background in small business. They had already owned a side business for a while. They bought into a really good franchise. Or they already had all of the skill sets they needed to make their new business a success.

For others, Plan B hasn't really worked out. Crucial business skill sets such as marketing, sales or the ability to influence others were insufficient or nonexistent. Customers were elusive. Funds didn't last as long as needed. Credit and home equity and the value of the stock portfolio all evaporated in the aftermath of 2008.

Although mortgage rates are at historic lows, the Plan B business owner can't refinance or get an additional loan for her business. The business cash flow might be working, but she can't show contracts that guarantee future revenues. For mortgage workouts even to be considered, infinite documentation is required, including even the advertising pages of bank statements with no financial information on them. If you didn't send that, please resend everything! By the time all the requested info is submitted, resubmitted and re-resubmitted, another month (or two or six) has gone by. Now bank statements, P&L statements and various affidavits required "for the underwriters' review" are needed for these new months that have passed.

Banks are sitting on money earmarked for small business loans, insisting on extremely rigorous qualifications even for established businesses, never mind a start-up or someone with less than two years of profitable operations.

Does this sound like you? The kids are in college

or just about ready to start. Increased life expectancy means you have another 20 or 30 or 40 years ahead of you. Plan A failed, Plan B hasn't gone as expected— the ship has run aground. What's next?

This book is for those of you who are moving on. The Formerly Corporate™, and I am one of them, have a choice: You can stay stuck right where you are, without a corporate job, without a viable business and without a viable plan. Or you can change something. If you are serious about making the small business you started in Plan B a success, and if you are serious about providing for your family and about re-funding your investment accounts for the later stage of life, this book is for you. I'll tell you how to move from Plan B to Plan C. That's where you, as Formerly Corporate™, become a Conquering Entrepreneur.

CHAPTER 1
Different Universe, Different Game

The first day of your new business

Let's say you managed a $1.5 million department in your corporate job. Not huge, but with a dozen or so employees to deal with, internal customers and some cross-functional responsibilities. You had a boss, some peers in other departments, some structure to your time and a paycheck that showed up every two weeks.

There were challenges, certainly: corporate politics, personnel squabbles, getting the department's job done. You probably thought it was pretty tough—until you moved from Corporate Way to Main Street.

Now let's say you are Formerly Corporate™ and starting a business for yourself. The Small Business

Administration has traditionally called a business small if it has under $500 million in revenue. Compared to Walmart or Google, that is small. Another group of small to mid-sized businesses fall in the $2 to 20 million range. These owners have figured out a lot about running a business—a whole business. However, most small business start-ups never reach $1 million in revenue. In fact, there are contests, awards and other recognition for businesses that reach that milestone.

So let's say you'd like to run a $1.5 million business for yourself. Based on our comments above, this would be a substantial small business. You ran that department, right? In fact, you ran it very well, with high productivity, stellar quality and excellent returns on the corporation's investment. So what can be so hard about becoming a small business owner?

I bet this is what you imagined Plan B would look like: Provide a fascinating product or service you are passionate about, no boss, no pesky competitors vying for the next promotion, fewer employee headaches, customers flocking in, more time to do what you like and profits that are all yours.

No boss! It's your business. That's so attractive to many new entrepreneurs that it's often the driving force for taking the leap of faith. That faith in yourself reflects your confidence, your enthusiasm, and your willingness to take risks.

No peers. No pesky competition for the next promotion from the department head next to you.

Fewer employees. Maybe none at all. You can

use freelancers, or independent contractors. Just when you need them. Just the ones you want. You'll be able to choose who to work with, not have them thrust upon you.

Flocks of customers. You know the kind of people you'd like to work with, the "ideal target" for your business. You know where they congregate. They will find you and be eager to do business with you.

Your time is now your own. True, you can arrange to play golf or attend the kids' activities. If others are working on your behalf, so much the better. You may arrange your business so working mothers can bring their infants to work, like a friend who built and sold The Natural Baby Company in the 90s. Or plan to work the 4-hour workweek like Tim Ferris.

All this is possible, but there's a lot more to it than meets the eye.

Reality is setting in

The boss may have had a bigger picture for what you could achieve, and some coaching skills and connections to help you achieve it. She might have challenged you to stretch, to learn, to try new things.

Without peers, there's no one to run things by, and no go-to person for the expertise you never developed when you worked in a distributed responsibility setting such as a corporation.

Without employees you have to do everything yourself. With them you have to pay their full salaries, benefits, and taxes. There's a sea of regulations to navigate, and *you* are now the HR department–along with all your other duties, of course.

The paycheck that goes to your employee every other week is now your responsibility. You have to get revenues to fund it, then write it and mail it yourself (unless you have wised up and hired a payroll service to do it). Your own check may not show up at all! Or stay in the desk drawer uncashed, in order to keep the ship afloat.

Has anyone said to you that all you need is the first client, and that once that happens, referrals will come streaming in? Not so much. Encouraging people to refer business to you is a skill and an art form. You need to develop it. And remember the "no competitors" thrill? True, they are not at your elbow in the workplace. They are at the same places you go, vying for your prospects.

Structuring your time turns out to be crucial. What to do first, then next? Modern life has been called ADD-inducing. The personality traits of many entrepreneurs lean in that direction anyway. Setting priorities and clear goals and sticking to them require focus, which is hard to maintain. "You're not the boss of me!" becomes a hollow cry.

And profits may be hard to find.

Having rebelled against the boss, the structure, the peers and the workers, many small business owners find they have to replace all of those functions to become successful in business. This may be why executive and business coaching, peer advisory groups and co-working spaces have become growth industries in the 21st century. It's lonely at the top.

The small business owner lives in a different universe from corporate America. Contrary to the recent Supreme Court decision, corporations are not persons. And the people who work on Corporate Way have no idea what life on Main Street is like. I heard an experienced small business owner say once, "So you managed $1.5 million *that someone else gave you?*"

Big deal, was his unstated implication. Go bring it in yourself and manage it. Then we can talk.

If you are a Formerly Corporate™ person now in business for yourself, you have a brilliant opportunity to shine in a new society, and a lot to learn. If Plan A was your first career, and Plan B was the first business you started or the first business model you tried, **Plan C is what you do now with all that you've learned and digested.** It's what you do next, now that everything is different.

So just what is your Plan C?

It is your new plan to build a better business. Using the successes and failures you already have under your belt, Plan C means getting real about the rules of the game and building the team you need–not just to play that game, but to win it!

The Conquering Entrepreneur plays the Plan C game for real—for real money, for real influence, for real impact.

A next step, a new decision for your business, lies

just in front of you. You see a crisis. You see an opportunity. Perhaps your customers are too few or your employees too many. Perhaps you've come across a possibility that requires you to invest money you don't have in hand. Perhaps your partner wants to pull out. Perhaps you have so much business you have to hire—but who? And for what position first?

It's exciting. It's frightening. It's necessary to change. For your business to succeed, you need to rethink, retool and, most importantly, reengage yourself. What's next?

Given all you've learned from Plan A and Plan B, it's time to strike out in a new direction for the next phase of your business.

What are your thoughts at this point? They probably range from "I'll do it!" to "I can't do it" and back again. But you must make a decision.

BASED ON WHAT? That is the key question. Whatever the decision, you know this:

The old rules, from the old game, don't apply, at least not directly. You have smacked right into the mindset shifts you'll need on your way to becoming a Conquering Entrepreneur:

- Your corporate experience is worth less (and more) than you think.
- You're playing a new game with new rules.
- Entrepreneur Land will be lonely if you let it.

SECTION TWO
Major Mind-Shifts Ahead

*Your corporate experience is worth less
(and more) than you think*

CHAPTER 2
Changing Your Formerly Corporate™ Outlook

Let's consider how you can approach your business challenges from two viewpoints: Your Formerly Corporate™ outlook (we'll call that your *FCO* for short) and what you need to learn to develop a successful Plan C and become a Conquering Entrepreneur.

FCO: My corporate experience *connects directly* to small business needs.

If you attempt to directly connect all of your corporate experience to your new world of Main Street, you will often encounter a mismatch. As a Conquering Entrepreneur you need to use the skills you learned in the corporate world in ways that you haven't anticipated. You'll need new skills as well as some guidance on what these skills are and which you need to learn first and practice the most.

Think about it from this point of view: What if you were an expert field hockey player who wanted to switch to ice hockey? You need to take all of the stick-handling skills you learned on the field, but now you have to do it all on ice, and much faster, and while skating backward!

Here's a more straightforward example: That corporate skill of managing a budget that you were so good at? That still needs to be done. But now, to manage a budget you first have to build that budget. It's Formerly Corporate™ to add or cut 10% to last year's budget that you inherited from your predecessor. It takes the thinking of a Conquering Entrepreneur to build a budget from scratch.

And where does the money to manage come from anyway? To bring in money, you need to sell. If you weren't in sales in your corporate job, you now must learn to sell–something that someone wants to buy.

FCO: I know about taking risks.

You may consider yourself a risk-taker. You wouldn't be reading this book if you didn't. But the risks are much...riskier when you're in the Plan B and C worlds. In fact, that may be just what you've realized if you're moving from Plan B to Plan C.

It's really RISKY out here. It was risky years ago, before 9-11 and before the great meltdown of 2007 to whenever it's over. But now it's worse. When you held your corporate job, you might have been risking your reputation at work by making a mistake. You might not get the next promotion. Or you might get a smaller raise. You might even lose your job, but you knew there were others to be had out there.

In your own business, you risk the house and your retirement funds and the kids' education. **That's really risky.**

Some people in the corporate world had enough power that they risked other people's jobs with the decisions they made. The more power you had in your corporate life, the greater the chance that you risk fooling yourself with the mind-shift from Corporate Way to Main Street. On Main Street the game is different–you don't know what you don't know.

FCO: You think you know "the game." But the game is not the same.

Think about the corporate focus versus your entrepreneurial focus. In the former, the focus was inward, about group process and aligning goals across the corporation. In the Plan C world, it's about the outside—specifically the customer, and opportunities to find and serve that customer. No matter what level you attained in your former world, you are now directly connected to your customer.

FCO: I know what it takes to win.
Define winning.

In the corporate world, winning is often *systems driven:* How to improve market share, or profit margins, how to beat the analysts' predictions, how to get too big to fail.

In the entrepreneur's world, you must first define the game. Then how to keep score. And then the rules. What game are you playing? Is it a win if you put points on the board or score a run? Is a win checkmate, or going out first? Or maybe the game is a bullfight—you or the bull. Who will still be standing after the fight?

In Plan C, the entrepreneur's win is *market driven*. Get customers, get cash flow! One of the major shifts from a Plan B business to a Plan C business is the realization that all the cool marketing in the world does you *no good without sales*. You may say, "no, duh!" to that. But many entrepreneurs just don't seem to get it. One of my own mentors, Suzanne Evans, has build a seven figure, Plan C business by helping entrepreneurs get just that message. If most entrepreneurs understood not only the need, but also how to get those sales, Suzanne would be out of business!

Systems have their place, but not without cash flow. You can't measure market share or profit margins without sales.

So define winning for yourself. I guarantee it will have something about gross revenues in it. When I ask people to set a financial target for themselves, $10,000 a month comes up often. It's a nice round number, it would provide a comfortable life here in the New York metropolitan area (but nowhere near an upper middle class lifestyle), and Formerly Corporate™ middle managers kind of feel like that's the least they deserve.

Or your target might be to pay the college tuition. If you have a partner to carry the living expenses, you might need $3,000 a month to pay a private school— better increase that for extras. That's for one kid in school at a time...

You might set a sales target instead. "I need twelve or four or two sales a month." Or it could be in terms of daily, weekly or yearly sales. The larger the average sale, the fewer the number needed, and the longer the sales cycle, the longer the time frame to measure across.

Once sales are happening and revenue is occurring, you've crossed a watershed. Once money is coming in, the next thing is to get more coming in than going out!

Then you can work on taking a salary, improving your profit margin and giving a portion of proceeds to those needier than you.

FCO: Business challenges just scale with size. Bigger business, bigger challenges.

But small business is not like big business...

I'm a chemical engineer by education, training and 30 years of (yes, corporate) oil company experience. Big Business. One of the things you learn in that field is to be concerned about scale. What works in the lab may not (make that, will not) work the same way in a commercial reactor. That's why we have pilot plants, sized between the lab equipment and the commercial reactor. As we test a process in the pilot plant, we learn things that weren't apparent in the lab—things like overheating and chunking up and plugging the exit lines, and...oh, you probably don't want to know. And then we test in the commercial reactor, too. We encounter the unexpected and work the kinks out. The commercial operators don't like to see the R&D folks come in with a new idea. It is likely to shut down their reactor and their production, and they get measured on their production, so shutting down is not good, so please go away, R&D. That's short-term thinking—how will we get to the next big thing, if we can't test it at a real scale?

But I'm also a chemist—my first degree, and I worked in the esoteric field of catalysis, where we thought on molecular, atomic and subatomic levels about what was going on in those reactions that the chemical engineers were trying to control in the scale-up process. It was scale-down thinking. Nano-thinking.

And here's a paradox of business scale. What works for big business doesn't just scale down to a small business.

Size matters

A lot has been written about microbusinesses, microloans and sole proprietor businesses (often women-owned) in Third World countries. The Bangladeshi economist Muhammad Yunus and his Grameen Bank garnered a Nobel Prize in 2006 for pioneering a new category of banking known as micro-credit, which grants small loans to poor people who have no collateral and who do not qualify for conventional bank loans.

I'd like to make a distinction here between micro (just smaller businesses) and Quantum Businesses.

Quantum Business can be understood as a business whose very small size means that it responds differently than a larger business would. In the same way that a very thin layer of copper cools off when electricity runs through it, while a thicker layer or wire heats up, a Quantum Business might have a counter-intuitive reaction.

This idea came up again from a business mentor, Art Radtke. Art uses the example of changing customer service approaches—a big business will use focus groups, test markets and amass mounds of data before implementing a major change, such as posting nutritional content in a fast food restaurant menu. A Quantum Business doesn't need to take the time to set up a focus group or amass data to study. The owner of a neighborhood candy shop wants to see if she gets more repeat business if she personally greets each customer as he or she come in. She doesn't need a focus group. She makes the decision and implements it that day. Over the next few weeks she keeps a record of how many repeat customers she has.

Neither approach is better or worse—just more appropriate for the situation. The market research approach is good for bigger business, and the ad hoc experiment is good for the Quantum Business. Both used their resources appropriately to seek an advantage while mitigating their risks. It's too risky for big business to change without testing, and too risky for Quantum Businesses to spend money for market research.

Be mindful of the scale of your business. Even if you intend to grow to a much larger business, when you're starting out, the game is different.

FCO: There's a great unmet need, and I've got the answer for it.

(I'm particularly sensitive to this one, since I spent 30 years in R&D and new product development, looking for the next great thing.)

Do you believe that "if I build it, they will come?" That customers are just waiting for you to show up in the marketplace?

That sounds naive, doesn't it? You wouldn't really say that out loud. But honestly, you might have just a touch of this idea lurking around. Self-talk can go like this:

"I know what I'm doing, I did it very well before; I managed an umpty-ump million dollar budget, I got good reviews and promotions. My target market doesn't even know what it's missing. I know what they should value, and I can get them to see why they should value my stuff, my offerings, my expertise, my brilliance. As soon as they know I'm there..."

In fact, your target market defines the value. You don't. You may have "built it," but they are not waiting to *find out about **you.***

They are looking for what they **want or need**, not **you specifically**. If they come across you in their search, they may pause to see if you fit. Unless you are really clear and crisp about how you can serve the need that they have *in the moment,* they will keep right on searching and asking till they find someone who can deliver.

Now unless your corporate career was in marketing, you need new skills here. And, if you *were* in marketing, you have to get over the notion that you can do everything your old department did. In either case, here are three phrases about marketing to point you in the right direction: *Market research. Market approach. Market capture.*

Market research.
Who do you want to do business with?

Defining and describing your target audience is a crucial step that new entrepreneurs too often gloss over.

For example, there's an elusive group of business owners out there that lots of people want to reach: the owner of a $2 to 50 million business with 5 to 25 employees. That's easy to say. You may even get a list from your local business librarian. That can be very helpful, but it's a bigger business kind of approach. How would you get their attention?

When I ask people to name five people in this category who would take their call, they freeze. That's a Quantum Business kind of market research.

Market approach.
Getting in front of your target market

Face-to-face contact. Find ways to meet people. As for elevator speeches—forget 60 seconds. You have about seven. So leave out your name and what you do. What can you say about how you helped clients, in seven to ten seconds? That works much better. If you intrigue them, they'll *ask* your name.

Referrals. Your best source will be your current clients. If you target your current customers and answer their needs, you'll get more of the same. There is nothing wrong with that, and it can provide a base income for you.

But if your business is viable but not optimal, moving up in terms of customer size, sophistication or just plain revenues is one good way to increase your business. Those prospects need more services and can pay more. Find out from your next desired level of customers what *they* need.

Social media savvy. Overwhelming as they may seem, the big four of the day (Facebook, LinkedIn, Twitter and YouTube) are just modern ways to touch and stay in touch with your prospects and customers. Do what you can, but find a balance. And don't forget your website in the social media frenzy.

Market Capture.
Addressing your target audience

Do your marketing materials reflect the needs you serve and the pain relief that you are able to provide to your target market?

Get the basics in place. Your message, your contact management, your outreach programs and your sales process.

Create a crisp and compelling message that says what you offer and why you are the one to choose. You must have one. The shorter you want your message to be, the harder it is to create it. How many focus groups and marketing gurus do you think it took Nike to come up with "Just do it"?

Create magnetic sales copy. Unless you're a skilled copywriter, please get help with this. Those looooong online sales letters we love to hate? They work for a lot of people.

There are many excellent freelance copywriters for hire. Ask friends whose marketing materials attract you who they used. If you want to stay stateside with your team, you can find many options. Some of them are Formerly Corporate™, like you. Add them to your team. If you search abroad, there are many brilliant writers, graphic designers, website techies and virtual assistants available to help you as well. Organizations such as o-Desk.com, Fiverr.com and the International Virtual Assistants Association (ivva.com) are good places to search for freelance services from all over the world.

Stay in touch with people you meet and people who reach out to you. To do that, you need to keep track of them. Pay attention to your website traffic and social media traffic. Keep up a current database of your clients, prospects, former customers, alliances and interesting people.

The more you can systematize and automate, the easier it will be to be consistent with staying in touch. Consistency is key. Newsletters, postcards, invitations to events, auto-responder emails—these are just a few ways to stay top of mind with your clients and prospects. If you need help getting started with these, try Constant Contact, Send-out Cards and aweber.com.

Go to www.formerlycorporate.com/C2-D4mktg for help outlining your market approach.

Become willing to sell

You may not have done any marketing and selling in your corporate job. In fact, you HATE selling. If you wanted to be a salesman, there are retail jobs paying $9 an hour. You could have done that.

You don't want to be a pest. You wish they would just buy so you wouldn't have to sell. There must be another way. Nope.

This is not a sales book, though you will have to learn to sell. But I will paraphrase a lesson I learned from reading and listening to the Great Sales Trainer, Zig Ziglar:

If you have something of value to offer a prospect and you don't make the offer, you are withholding that value from them. You are denying them the option of deciding for themselves.

And I would add, if you don't have something of value to offer or are not willing to offer it, you might be in the wrong arena. Most businesses fail. Most Formerly Corporate™ people find the transition too hard. Blunt advice here: You have to sell something. Offer goods or services that people want to buy, or get out of business.

Are you still with me? Good, then let's get out that icky place I just left you in. You need new resources: Which ones, and where are they?

FCO: Who is the go-to person on this need I have? Get 'em in here!

In Plan C, there's less snapping of fingers– "There, that's done!" You were used to having someone else take care of "that." Now, you need skills in your business that you don't have time to develop, or the inclination to develop them, either. Your best move is to find good team members.

I often say the two things I miss most about corporate life are the steady paycheck and the IT department. When I learned to sell what someone else wanted to buy, the paycheck arrived. When I found the right IT expert (another small businessperson) who would come and fix my computer quickly and reliably, I was ecstatic! I had an IT department.

Finding the right teammates, and the right resources, is harder when you have to find and choose them on your own. When, how and whom to hire are much harder decisions in small business than they were in your corporate life.

Looking ahead to Chapter 4, there's a hidden opportunity here: You can help yourself while you are helping another business owner.

The major mindset shifts

Plan B was only the first iteration. You learned a lot. Some things worked—many did not. Are you still trying to the play the old game? You may feel as if you've lost your bearings in this new one. For Plan C, you need a rulebook, a coach, a scout—maybe a quarterback. You need to identify whether you're playing on a field, a court, a board or a card table.

Your task is not to go into the world to "bless" your prospects and clients with your vast corporate knowledge and experience. Your challenge is to enter their world, not entice them into yours.

Let's take a deeper look at those big mindset shifts.

CHAPTER 3
You Know More
(and Less) than You Think

If, when you first leave your job or start your business, you try to apply your corporate experience directly to your new small business, you are in trouble.

Would you guess at the number of people I've met, from marketing gurus to sales stars to team champions, who've come out of corporate life and said some version of, "in my new business, I will bring the strategies, tools and techniques of the (name their industry and function) to the small business owner, and bless them with my knowledge, vast experience and savvy, at a price they can afford."

If I had a nickel for every time I've heard that, as my mother would say, I'd be rich.

The experienced small business owner can smell

Formerly Corporate™ people a mile away. So even if they could use the services you are selling, they'll shy away because they know a few things you don't know.

Corporate experience is valuable, don't get me wrong. But with *only* corporate experience, you see a mere fragment of the whole business of "being in business for yourself." You look through the lens of your big company experience, and you assume the picture will clear up momentarily.

Here are a few blank spots in your view of your new business:

Finding the resources you need in the entrepreneurial environment is different and more difficult than it was in the corporate world.

Depending on what position you held, you might have asked a colleague, a subordinate or your executive team for information you needed, equipment required or help to launch a new product or division. "Find it, fix it, or make it happen," you declared, and voila! It was done.

As the top dog in your own business, you may be the only dog. Although you may be skilled at delegating, there is no one to delegate to. Although you need a website that wows, your website building skills don't measure up. Although you need marketing copy for that website, you are not the best copywriter, by far.

You may think that if you can't hire those people as employees, you can't have those services. You may think that if you don't have revenues to support them, you have to do everything yourself. Those are fallacies of the Plan B mindset.

Learn to work with a different kind of network

It's not that the resources you need aren't there. It's just that obtaining them requires a different kind of network than you had in your corporate job, one you may have rarely experienced.

Let's talk about what a business network is, from some new perspectives. My definition of a network is that it is *your connections with people who may send you referrals, collaborate with you on some projects, and support your business with services you need or buy your services*. Note that I list the buyer last. The sale comes after the connections are made.

To quote Dr. Ivan Misner, founder of Business Network International (BNI®), the largest business network organization in the world:

"Your Network, with a capital N, is a systematically and strategically selected group of people on whom you can call as the need arises. It is a diverse, balanced and powerful system of sources— people from all facets of the business world—that will provide the referrals, knowledge, and support you need in key areas of your business or profession."[4]

Bob Burg defines the activity of networking as

---

[4] *Business by Referral, Ivan R. Misner and Robert Davis, Bard Press, 1998, p. 29*

"cultivating mutually beneficial, give-and-take, win-win relationships."[5]

If you are now in a Main Street kind of business, whether retail, franchise, or service provider, you'll need to have connections within your local community.

If you are building a virtual business, say an online sales or online information marketing business, you will need to build connections with people who are willing to share their lists or co-market a product with you.

If you are a budding entrepreneur who will need financing to take your business to a buy-out or IPO, you will need to have connections within the angel and venture capital communities.

If you are a candidate for public funding, such as a new technology business or manufacturing who will need significant numbers of skilled workers, you will need to learn how to do business with the government.

Here are ten ways you can build a network that will support the business you want to have, not that Plan B business you're moving away from.

1. Actively participate in trade associations where your target market belongs, so you meet targeted prospects. Subscribe to the many free or low cost newsletters and distribution lists

---

[5] *Bob Burg, Endless Referrals, McGraw-Hill, 1999, p. xvi*

that their event organizers maintain.

2. Join a hard-referral group such as Business Network International (bni.com), to help you build a "sales force" of referral partners.

3. Join and contribute to a professional association in your field, so you stay sharp and up-to-date.

4. Become active in a local business association or Chamber of Commerce, so you meet both local resources and local prospects.

5. Blend both face-to-face and virtual networking.

6. Look to social media and virtual support services, so you expand your network.

7. Find out who the online leaders in your area of expertise are. Follow them, subscribe to their lists and interact with them on social media. Go to their events.

8. Look for organizations that coach entre-preneurial CEOs in the tools, tactics and techniques of building a bullet-proof, fundable business plan.

9. Observe who the connectors and influencers in your business community are. Hint: They may not be the bright, shiny marketing types. Help them.

10. Find a mastermind group. There are other business owners like you who are eager to share and learn from mutual experiences—both best and worst practices!

Relationship dynamics are different, too

There's a reason coffee shops are so popular with small business owners. Independent business people don't need to be lone rangers. Call up another businessperson and buy him a cup of coffee. Ask how he handled a particular problem. If it's a bigger deal, or a more influential person, invite her to lunch. If you play golf, now's the time to take a few lessons. The reason business people play golf, aside from liking the game, is that it's a very good way to get to know whether those in the foursome are people you'd like to do business with.

One difference between corporate and small business life is this: In your corporate life a coffee was a break, or wasted time in the corporate halls. In your new world, the coffee shop is part of the workplace, and you are working when you meet people from your network there.

Online networking has become more and more important. By interacting with online connections and adding valuable information and insights to questions and comment pages, you are building a *personal* relationship with experts and authorities in your field —even if you have never met them face-to-face. You are also building your own reputation as an authority in your field. Like going to the coffee shop to meet with local connections, the time you spend building real connections with real people online is a good investment in your business.

Here's a combined focusing and productivity tip: Block some recurring "coffee-date" times in your calendar. If you don't have an actual face-time meeting then, use that time to connect with someone in your online world. You'll be reminded that you need to do these on a regular basis, and you'll have the time committed for it.

There's gold in who you know & what you know

This point leads back to my earlier suggestion that you should find out who the influencers and connectors (I/C) are in whichever community you operate. Your first step should then be to *help them*. It's not fair to ask for their connections without first finding out what they need. This does not necessarily require cash, but it certainly requires sensitivity and reciprocity.

Here are several places to look.
❑ In your local community
❑ In the online community
❑ In the investment community
❑ In the government sector

For example, in your local community, you might sponsor a school sports team that an I/C supports. You might volunteer in a charitable organization where that person also invests time. You might organize a group of people from your own network to build awareness of local businesses. These types of activities will insure that you draw the attention of those YOU wish to influence, and they will become

47

curious about you and your business. Then *they* will ask *you*–and that is much better than you pushing yourself on them.

Start out online and identify a few I/Cs you'd like to make personal connections with. Build up a relationship there. In comments on their websites, make helpful suggestions or point to resources. Repost or retweet *their* materials. Broaden *their* audiences by introducing them to your network. Don't push *your* wares. The good ones will eventually reciprocate. After a while, you can ask for an in-person connection. Do you know anyone who could introduce you personally? I've found that I/Cs are often open to a phone call or Skype meeting IF you've been contributing to their online community.

What *you* might find very easy (making phone calls, building web pages, writing fund-raising letters or organizing a team of volunteers) could be very valuable to the person you are trying to connect with.

Learning to do business with the government also requires significant new skills. While relationships are still crucial, there are many rules, written and unwritten, about how to approach a government entity for business opportunities. One good place to start is with your local Small Business Development Center (SBDC) branch. These SBDCs, part of the US Small Business Administration, offer advice and counsel to new and established small businesses. State governments also provide introductions to doing business with state and federal entities, usually through the state departments of labor. These are your tax dollars at work, and they often offer courses in how to do business with the government.

There are for-profit organizations that help as well. Here again, people have invested a lot of time, energy and money in developing connections and mapping the maze of government access. Money spent with them can really accelerate your trip through that maze. (I'm not talking about pay-to-play, here, or buying access in other nefarious ways. I'm talking about legitimate consultants who've been around and can help you avoid detours and dead-end. They are out there—ask your network to help you find them.

In New Jersey, for instance, UCEDC.com provides advice, microloans and training in accessing the world of government contracting. Another resource for small business loans is the Regional Business Assistance Corporation (RBACloan.com).

If you are comfortable in this arena, by all means continue to build new relationships and strengthen older ones. You may even find a business opportunity in helping others do the same.

If you aren't familiar with this game, finding knowledgeable sources as well as a mentor will be crucial for your successful venture into government contracting. After a few forays into this world (I had a goal one year early in my consulting business to learn how to do business with the federal government), I realized the learning curve was too steep and too time-intensive for me. But that's me, and if you have a head start, this can be a very lucrative source of business.

Other people's money

As a budding entrepreneur whose scale of business will require other people's money, relationship building is Job Number One.

In the angel and venture capital world, you never know who has a checkbook in their pocket. I've seen people write $100,000 checks to an entrepreneur they just met—although the meeting was not a random one! Introductions are gold, and finding and cultivating the people who can make those introductions is the art of this world.

Beware: Cold calling and randomly pitching for money really doesn't work here, and can kill your chances on the spot. Learn where, how and with whom you can safely study how to hold yourself out for a qualified investment. Many such organizations exist.

You can earn the respect of your local investment community by building a plan to raise funds in addition to your "Fund-raising Plan." That's not just a play on words.

Before hitting the circuit, as it's called, with requests for large chunks of money, the savvy entrepreneurial CEO seeks advice from selected people who can, in turn, make specific and qualified introductions to accredited investors and selected professional service providers (attorneys, account-ants, bankers, executive coaches) who are experts in this specialized world. On this path, you can find excellent coaching so when you do begin to ask for funds, your pitch is well crafted and to the point.

There are local, non-profit organizations that offer education and information to entrepreneurs and investors alike, in every region. For example, here are six such organizations on the East Coast. Many are supported and/or sponsored by the 28-year-old non-profit educational and training organization led by Dan Conley, known as Entrepreneurs' University (entreuniv.org).

Similar and complementary organizations include
- MIT Enterprise Forum, with chapters worldwide (mitef.org)
- The 128 Innovation Capital Group in the Boston area (128cg.org)
- Venture Association of New Jersey (VANJ.com)
- NJ Entrepreneurs Network (www.njen.org)
- New Jersey Technology Council (NJTC.org)

If you are new to this world, go to one of the local meetings. Introduce yourself to the people in these organizations. Don't ask them for money. Ask them for help, and offer to help them. They know a LOT of people. It's the introductions you are after.

Takers and givers

You wouldn't believe how many business people completely blow the relationship dynamics at work in this approach. There are at least two ways to mess up.

First, some people, rather than see that they can trade something valuable for the other person's attention and help, expect the proverbial "something for nothing." They don't get very far, build few real relationships and conclude that referrals don't work. And they are right. Networking and referral-based marketing don't work very well for this type of person.

Some business owners often believe they **should not spend any money** for advice, although they've blown through their life savings as well as their families' and friends' investments trying to figure out how the game works. Therefore, they tend to take advantage of advisors, who offer instruction, guidance and introductions. This type of new entrepreneur is often so self-absorbed that he doesn't recognize a gift when he sees it, and complains bitterly when the "helping" folks expect payment (Cash? Stock? Warrants?) for their own time.

Consider this story. An entrepreneur with a "better mouse trap" (really) accepted coaching on his idea, his pitch, his business structure and his intellectual property. He learned quickly from a group of advisors, paying basically pocket money upfront to get started. As a result of that coaching and introductions made on his behalf, he won a "most fundable" designation at a local venture fair. When his own lack of full disclosure came to light, he resentfully refused to pay the accumulated costs for the coaching he had accepted.

Or here's another one: A small business owner met with a business advisor (ok, it was me). We had a lengthy discussion about his business, his transition from corporate life, his needs and some very specific and creative suggestions for how he could better market his health care business. Then he stood up, and declared, "There is zero, that is zero dollars, value in this kind of talk for my business. I would never waste the time or write a check for this kind of conversation."

On his way out the door, he said, "I'm putting my marketing person to work on that marketing scheme right away."

People talk, so you won't be able to hide this kind of behavior.

You expect people to pay you for the services you provide. Make sure that you pay for the services you receive.

I see a second and a more insidious problem in over-giving. We hear so much about the rewards of giving: From the golden rule to BNI's 'Givers Gain' philosophy to Bob Berg's best-seller *The Go-Giver*, generosity is extolled. And don't get me wrong—I believe in being generous and helping others.

However, you know what the phrase "giving away the store" means, right? On a visceral level, it resonates because you may have either done it or taken advantage of someone who did. Reluctant to claim what she deserves after having built a sturdy network of valuable connections, the "over-giver" suffering the lack of reciprocity eventually gets

53

discouraged. Relationships fester. Actually the resentment builds in both giver and receiver and gnaws away at hard-won relationships.

We recognize the greedy takers more easily than the over-givers. Which are you? Or are you both?

Reap what you sow

It takes patience to find the right people and to build mutual respect and willingness to help each other with your business. But patience and urgency are two sides of the same coin when it comes to successful business. Sometimes you need the patience to urgently kiss a lot of frogs—to work through the possibilities and to find the right people to work with, the right resources for your team.

Learn to ask for reciprocity. Ask for business, ask for referrals, ask to go along to someone else's business or trade group. Let people introduce you for a change. When you've sown the seeds for good business relationships, and tended the garden diligently, remember to harvest your crop.

Then take it to market and sell it.

CHAPTER 4
The Starburst Business™ Model

We talked earlier about Quantum Businesses, those companies that are small enough that the "normal rules or laws of business" operate differently. I want to distinguish these types of businesses from the proverbial "mom and pop" business.

In broad strokes, what business models do we have to choose from?

1. The multinational corporation (hey, they all started somewhere).
2. The regional corporation (many medium-sized banks are here, as are some multi-paper news organizations and locally owned restaurant groups.)
3. The cooperative business (Cabot Farms, Woodfern Shoprite supermarkets in the Northeast).

4. The franchise model, which combines 1 or 2 with a smaller footprint and perhaps local ownership of one or a group of franchise operations.
5. The consortium, a loose federation of like-minded people, using common methodologies and sharing best (and worst) practices.
6. The professional practice (attorneys, accountants, financial planners, consultants).
7. The mom-and-pop family business, which could be anything from restaurants to retail to insurance agencies.
8. The freelancer, or free agent, taking on project work for others using a specific skill set.
9. The solopreneur, one person doing the work with no desire for employees—EVER!

There is another business model emerging in these tough times of financial meltdown, vast uncertainty and the unrecognizability of the world economic models.

It may have been there all along, but it's becoming more and more visible—in fact, once you learn to recognize it, it becomes a bright object in the dark sky.

I call it the Starburst Business™. My favorite example is Open Door Publications, owned by Karen Hodges Miller. Full disclosure here—Karen's business model has developed partly under my tutelage—she's been a long-term client. And she and I co-authored a book, *Finish Your Book*. And she is the publisher of this book.

So you could think I'm too close to this example

(something Karen herself questioned).

Karen insisted for years that she didn't want employees, she didn't want helpers; she just wanted to write and edit and make some (not a lot) of money. She was Michael Gerber's quintessential E-myth Technician.[6]

But eventually she wanted to shift from just writing for others to helping people write and publish their own books. In the face of severe restructuring in the publishing business, with major houses disappearing and vanity presses moving from a pejorative "he had to publish it himself" to "print-on-demand" modernity, Karen wanted to become an independent book publisher!

One day in a mastermind team meeting, she was holding forth again as to why she didn't have or want a *business*. It was still too scary a concept. I jumped up, grabbed my markers and began to draw the Business Structure She Already Had!

---

[6] Gerber, Michael, The E-Myth Revisited, Harper Business, 2001, pp. 26-33.

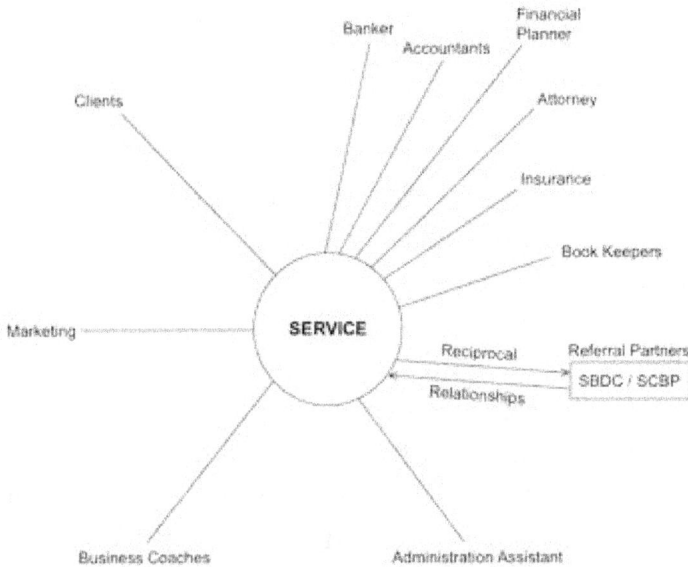

Banker
Accountants
Financial Planner
Clients
Attorney
Insurance
Book Keepers
Marketing
SERVICE
Reciprocal
Relationships
Referral Partners
SBDC / SCBP
Business Coaches
Administration Assistant

Figure 1 Starburst Business™ Model

A constellation of independent contractors—ghostwriters, copy writers, copyeditors, proofreaders, graphic designers, website designers, marketing companies, printers, public relations people—all trusted members of Karen's team but working for themselves (and with other clients—the IRS is picky about independent contractor status). All had skills required to serve her clients, but none were needed full time and none wanted to be an employee. She did have one part-time office assistant/layout and design specialist on payroll, but that person's replacement was (did you guess it?) a Starburst Business™ herself.

How is this different from ordinary sub-contracting? In the construction and contracting industry, it's common to work with many sub-contractors. And unfortunately, it's also common for those subs to be hard to manage, doing too many projects at once and/or missing in action.

In another example of subcontracting, consulting firms often use subcontractors to fulfill a large engagement. Or to bring in skills that the primary consultant doesn't have. Unfortunately, some just fill their website with accomplished and interesting people who reflect well on the primary consultant. But others such as Nano-biz, LLC have built international relationships and support structures to bring corporate business to the Formerly Corporate™. Nano-biz is in Starburst mode.

And as a third example, in a web design business, often the principal has one set of skills and needs to fill in with another. The business owner may be the technical type, who can code the site but is not the best at graphic design or writing copy. Or the owner might be the graphic designer, who sometimes needs sophisticated coding skills to complete a high value site for a customer willing to pay top dollar. In either case, they use photographers, copywriters, proofreaders and other complementary services to deliver a finished website to their client.

On the next page is an example of a Starburst Business™ model for a franchise business.

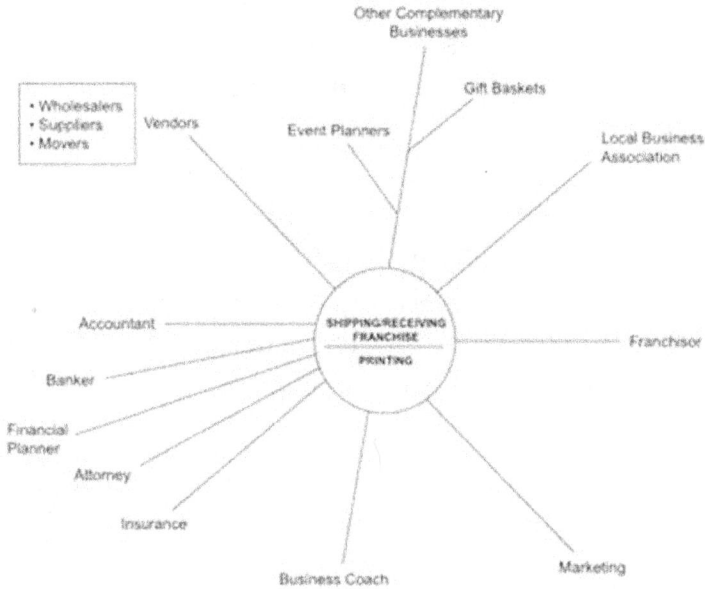

**Figure 2 Starburst Business ™ Model for
Shipping Franchise**

What distinguishes a Starburst Business™ from an ordinary subcontracting arrangement? Two things:

First, the intention to *collaborate as an association of equals.* The ancillary businesses are *necessary for* but *independent of* the core business. They bring required skills the core business could not function without. They support other core businesses as well, and may themselves be core to other Starburst Businesses™.

Second, the owners view the *relationship among the Starburst Businesses™ as strategic.* Another client—an award-winning kitchen and bath design firm, Aurora Kitchens and Interiors, views the starburst model as essential to their business development, and easier to manage than a traditional pyramid model with C-suite people, managers, and employees. Since they are in that infamous "evaporating contractor" world, they are making their mark as reliable, meticulous and personable, and seek out other contractors with complementary skills and *attitudes* to build their Starburst Business™. You can see in Figure 3 how this model continues to grow.

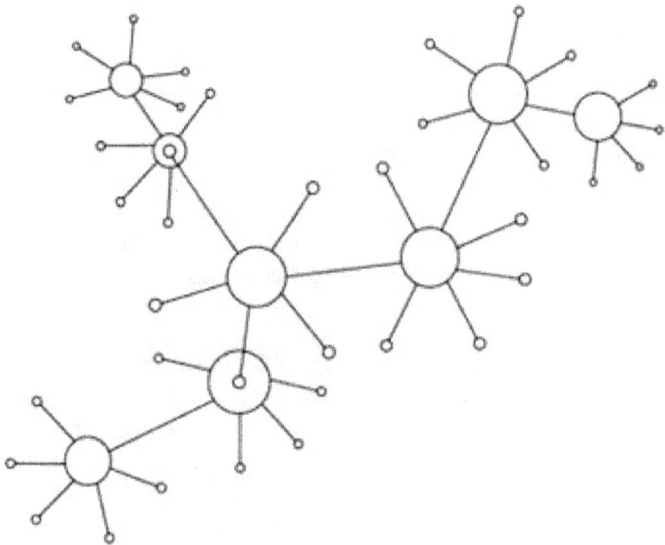

Figure 3 Starburst Businesses & Constellations

Networks of business alliances form, with business owners connecting to provide services the others need. Backlinks, to use an Internet term, form among the various businesses. As word spreads, good people and needed services are referred and shared among the Starburst Businesses™. For-profit and not-for-profit connections are made as people get to know one another in a more personal way. Connections expand and strengthen. A community forms.

Starburst: A 21st century business model

Rather than viewing the Starburst Business™ as just the old subcontracting model, we can think of it as the business model of the future. The corporate jobs of the 20th century evaporate daily. Large businesses are mired in a swamp of uncertainty and reluctance to make commitments to employees.

In a Starburst Business™, it is possible to scale a small business up without creating a big bureaucracy. How far is not clear—at some point, the benefits of the corporate structure will make sense. But Open Door Publications and Aurora Kitchens and Interiors and Nano-biz have contributed to the viability and growth of dozens of small business owners, not to mention their authors and homeowners and business clients who are served directly.

Is that job creation? Or something new? Is it even measured by current economic metrics?

CHAPTER 5
The new game you're playing

Imagine you had come to Earth from a far-distant galaxy. Not only would the situation in front of you be new and indecipherable, but when you looked up at the sky from our spot in the middle of the Milky Way, it would look different and disorienting as well.

Or imagine you had come to the USA from a different part of the world, from a different culture altogether, as many entrepreneurs, in fact, do. Navigating societal norms, not to mention traffic flow, would be daunting and confusing. In New Jersey, you have to turn right at a "jug-handle" before you can turn left. Who knew?

So here you are—a start-up in the world of small business. Having left the corporate life behind, you are doing this on your own. You're determined to be successful in your new milieu. How will you figure out the game? The first step is crucial.

Identify the game

Sunday afternoon on my first trip to London, we saw some people spread out over a field in a park with a bat and ball. I assumed they were playing baseball, what else? A closer look revealed a funny-looking bat—fat and short. You know already this was a cricket game. I watched for a while, asked some questions and left with some new and basic knowledge—this game might go on all day!

If you are new to small business, you need to find the game, and watch it for a while.

Observe the play

First, go to where the game is played. One of your tasks is to develop new business. Therefore, you find out where your target market gathers, and figure out the rules of engagement with them.

You may be approaching a target market where you have plenty of skills and credibility. If you've left your corporate job and started a business providing expertise and services to that market, you know a lot about the game. You just don't know what it feels like to be on the other team or the other side of the desk, and how much work all those salespeople had done before they showed up in front of you, the decision maker. Now you're the petitioner, and the rules of the game don't favor you. Watch the play.

Note: In my business some prospects can be found at the local business events. But my best targets (owners of businesses between $1 and $20 million in revenue) don't go to business card exchanges or after-work meet-and-greets. One main reason is that they are targets there, and they don't like being shot at!

Too many people are trying to sell them services they may already have or have decided about—insurance, investment advice, employee benefit services, real estate or network marketing opportunities. Those are relationship-based services as well, and a successful businessperson already has relationships with providers of those services. They are unlikely to throw their current provider overboard just because someone pressed a business card in their hand and said, "Call me!"

What if you are one of the sellers of insurance, investment advice, or other services or opportunities? You will find more success when you find out where your target prospects do spend time, and go there. For instance, if you have an insurance business and know of a carrier that will take on horse farms for a great price, do some research, find out where the "Equine Stabling Association of North America" is and go to their convention. (I just made that name up but there is an association for everything you could think of, and things you couldn't make up if you were trying!). Take a look at the Association of Association Executives or at www.Weddles.com/associations, a website for extensive lists of United States and international associations.

Your local reference librarians can be your best friends in this search. It's their job, and they love nothing more than to have someone ask a challenging question. Your state may have a specialized business library. With so much online now, it's not hard to find great resources and guidance from many sources.

If you plan it right, you may be the only person in your profession to be talking to a room full of the right people for you. Now that would be a real advantage! Your competitors are back at the general networking event, tugging on sleeves, and you? You might even get to be the speaker (aka the expert) in a roomful of prospects.

When you move to Conquering Entrepreneur, you've already developed some knowledge and skills. Now you're trying to move up from the minors. Watch from the sidelines for a while. See what the professional-level players do. Imitate them. Take lessons. Practice. Expand and polish your skills.

A crucial question: Is it realistic to be a solo-preneur in the field you've chosen? What other services will enable you to deliver on your promises? Perhaps a Starburst Business™ is a better approach.

If you have moved into a completely new field—you were an accountant but are now exercising the other side of your brain and doing interior design—there are rules you don't even know about. They're stacked against you all right, and you may be clueless. How will you decipher the new game?

Study the rules

Let's start with developing a business network in your new world. Why?

First, because this is how you will learn who the people are who know the rules of your new game. You can, and should, learn who the experts in your field are—who wrote the book about it. Go to hear them speak. Buy their books and courses. But how to find someone who will share what they wish they'd done differently in their first year of business, or introduce you to the right people, or take your call when you're stuck? That's not as easy as going to the business section on the bookstore.

The people you are looking for are not standing there with a rulebook in their hands. They won't be listed as "guru to the newbie" in an online search. But between you and that exalted expert, there are people who are on the ground, in your city, who have a give-back attitude, and would be willing to help you. *As much as you need prospects and clients for your business, you also need resources.* In the process of building a network, you will find some of them.

Second, because referral based marketing is a powerful strategy for the new business owner, and your pool of referral partners is the heart of your network. Those referral partners may help you in your own business, but they also allow you to help the people you are soliciting. Wouldn't you rather do business with someone who has helped you already?

In your Formerly Corporate™ life, a network was

often built in. Your company, your department, your trade association—when interacting there, you had a built-in place in the world. You were on the team already.

In this new game, you have to try out, to earn your spot. There are skills to learn—how to approach strangers, insert yourself into a group, talk about what you do. You need to find out what phrases and descriptions of your work people relate to.

You must *practice* until you master the art of networking. Then keep doing it. Ivan Misner, Ph.D., of Business Network International (BNI), talks about doing wind sprints—practicing the fundamentals of your game—just like athletes who practice whether they are on a high school team or in the pros.

The new business owner often starts with local networking venues such as a Chamber of Commerce, a service club or a group of professional peers. There are good reasons to do all. You build visibility and credibility, you build social capital by contributing to your community and you stay current with developments in your area of expertise.

Meeting with your professional peers is an excellent way to learn the latest new thing, keep up with developing trends, build your skills and enhance your credibility. When I started in business as a management consultant, I visited a local Chamber of Commerce meeting. There, I was invited to the local chapter of the Institute for Management Consultants. In that group, I learned how to be a professional management consultant. One of the topics we talked about a lot was how to approach target prospects. But there were few target prospects there.

While meeting with my peers was an important part of learning the rules, I also needed to discover where to find my prospects. That's where I could *really* observe the game.

Use the right equipment

In my cricket example, I had a few clues. There was a field, and a ball and a stick of some kind. It was the stick that first gave away what game I was watching. Think about the implications of playing with the wrong equipment or being in the wrong place. You wouldn't play chess with checkers, although the boards are similar. You can't play poker with a Go Fish deck or race horses around a NASCAR course.

In the Plan C world, you are playing a different game. You may not be on a field at all, but an indoor court. You may not play the new game with your trusty old baseball mitt; you may need a squash racket.

If you target small business owners, for example, some play on Main Street, but some play on Wall Street. The gear you need to work with the Main Street players will be different from the gear you need to work with start-up entrepreneurs.

In the Main Street business, the details are very different from corporate life. In retail, part of the equipment is inventory, which costs money to buy and hold. The rhythm of cash flow, though, is different from the rhythm of inventory. When a retail establishment makes all its "profit" after Black Friday, 11/12s of the way through the year, you could call the "gear needed" a cash cushion. Same for a service business such as elder care or financial investing—developing a prospect pool can take time, and in start-up phase, the advisor will need deep personal pockets to stay afloat. The Main Street guy will need stealth, cheap, guerilla marketing tactics, not the slick corporate marketing he may have been used to.

By a Wall Street business, I mean someone who is building a business that others will invest in through angel and venture capital and eventually stocks sold to the public. Whether the idea is a consumer product, a new software platform, a medical device or a new energy source, the money required is more than the inventor can come up with alone. The Plan B entrepreneur is often stuck in the details of how cool the idea or product is, how it will revolutionize a technology or cure cancer. I'm not kidding here—people are genuinely working on revolutionary technologies such as fusion energy or molecules to target specific cancers. There are a number of organizations throughout the country that offer information and coaching to start-up entrepreneurs. Some are targeted to specific fields, others are more general. In the Northeast there are GUST and Entrepreneurs University; in the Midwest there is the Kaufmann Institute for Entrepreneurship. There are others throughout the United States. Just Google "entrepreneurs" in your area and you will surely find an organization to assist you.

To move to Plan C though, the Wall Street wannabe will need a well-honed fund-raising pitch. That's a piece of equipment that she probably doesn't have yet, at least not the top-of-the-line variety. It needs to be vetted, polished and checked over by the "equipment managers," an experienced set of investors and advisors who know what this game is, what equipment is needed and how it is played.

Investors aren't always that interested in the details of the cool invention. They have a very narrow focus—what's in it for them?

They want to know:
- What problem you solve
- Who needs it
- How much money you want
- How much you've invested so far
- What you will do with their money
- By when
- Who's on your team
- When they will get their money back
- At what return on their investment

And they want to know it in two **or** five **or** ten minutes. Not two-to-five or five-to-ten. That's the game. Your pitch is the equipment. And just so you realize it, if you're looking for investors, that outline is worth way more than the price of this book and the time you've spent reading it so far.

Master the rules

Once you have identified the game, studied the rules and observed the play for a while, you have to master the rules. It can take days to play a cricket game. How do you win the damn game?

One of the rules of your new game is that business development is a perpetual task. In your business, do people go for an immediate sale? Is it retail, and focused on coupons and specials and impulse buys? You could be a luxury shop, where repeat purchases of expensive merchandise warrant a longer-term approach. Are you a service business, one where relationships need to be nurtured before the suggestion of doing business even comes up?

Here's an example that came up in a conversation with my Team Nimbus colleagues just the other day. We were talking about the strategy of getting involved with non-profit or service organizations to meet the movers and shakers who also donate their time. This is an approach often recommended to the new business owner—do good and you will do well, because you'll meet all these important people. In practice, people often get no business from these activities. Why? As Art Radtke pointed out: They are so cautious about not taking advantage of their more successful co-workers that they take no advantage of the situation at all. They don't ask for business, because they are unsure of the rules.

Of course, some business does get exchanged in

these situations, so we need to learn the rules rather than leave the game. I am an expert in my world *of referral-based marketing and peer coaching for small business owners.* But to attract bigger business clients, I've learned to ask people who've already done that: What are the rules here? How does this work—in this group of people, in this context?

Practice your skills

How do you develop new skills? I'm sure that most of you will say that someone taught you. An aunt who loved card games, an uncle who played chess with you, an older cousin who could outshoot you at the backyard hoop. They not only were willing to teach you the rules, but they *played the game with you.*

This is a crucial part of learning to play the new game. Find someone who will play the game **with** you—who will let you play in their game, even as a substitute, even as a ball girl. Are you starting over? Do you need to learn new skills? The basics? Are you doing OK but not as well as you expected?

Revisit the fundamentals. Ask questions. Shadow someone who's experienced and accomplished. Yes, if you are on Plan C, you may feel that you are beyond that stage of life. That you can figure it out for yourself. That you shouldn't need help. You are not alone but if you stay in that mindset, you'll stay stuck.

Did you know there's an Internships over Forty Program? Must be a demand for people willing to learn, and there must be others who are willing to learn. The best teacher is experience, and the best way to get experience is to play the game.

The third big blank

Beyond What Game Is This? and What Are the Rules Here?, there's a third question for the Plan C entrepreneur to answer:

What are you trying to create? Of the three main types of people in business for themselves, choose the one you are. Be honest with yourself. There is honor in each, but you cannot stand with a foot in all three.

1. In business, but really waiting for another job

This stance has given consultants a bad name. If your desire is to get another job, tell people that. How will they know otherwise? Even if people were able to read your mind, it's a waste of their energy and your social capital to keep them guessing. The win in this game is to build contacts and make inroads to find that job.

You will find more success in treating your job search as a full-time endeavor than by dividing your budget of time, energy and money between two objectives. And you will make a better impression and get better opportunities, if you have made a clear decision in your own mind.

When I decided to become a consultant, I started

telling people that my profession was management consultant. I didn't tell people that I was looking for an engineering position. I still tell people that I have a Ph.D. in Chemical Engineering from Princeton University and worked for Mobil for many years. It's all true, and it is the source of many experiences and some wisdom. But I am not looking for a job as an engineer. Or a job as anything. I'm a management consultant in my own practice.

See how clear that was?

If you can generate some cash flow on a temporary basis, by all means use your talents and resources to do that. If an opportunity comes up, at least look at it. And realize that the opportunity will come with a cost. There may be a cost to invest, a cost to move, an emotional cost of giving something up, a cost of losing another opportunity if you take the one in front of you.

If you want to run a sustainable, successful business, you'll need to put your heart into it. If you have to take a lesser status job to fund your business start-up, do that. But if you really want a job, do *that*.

2. Independent contractor

This is another viable approach, though it's limiting since time is traded for money, and there is only so much time. It's often a singles game, though that, too, is limiting.

Many Formerly Corporate™ folks become independent contractors, and it may work fine for you. You have a skill set that is marketable. You look for project work, often at companies like the one you left or through various freelance matching sites on the web. With no intention of building an enterprise (even a small one, with employees and payroll and personnel headaches! Ye gods!), you build yourself a job. Many have observed, notably Michael Gerber in his E-myth series, that one of the pitfalls of this approach is that you traded in your old bad boss (her) for your new worse boss (you!). And you've traded the stifling structure (or comforting boundaries) of the corporate environment for an endless stream of tasks without an end in sight.

You may find that either you have too much work, and therefore no time to market, or no work, and no marketing momentum built up. But many people find that freelance/independent contractor status suits them fine. They love their craft, are very good at it and master the work/marketing conundrum so they have a fairly dependable income stream.

A win here is finding repeat clients with interesting projects for whom you become the go-to person.

3. The Conquering Entrepreneur

The distinguishing feature of the Conquering Entrepreneur is the desire to make a bigger impact on the world.

If you have the mindset of the Conquering Entrepreneur, you want to make an impact. It may be a big impact: To cure cancer, solve the energy crisis, create jobs, provide medical care in third world countries, democratize the food supply, create the next big app.

It may be a more local impact: A restaurant group that supports sustainable farming in their area, or a law firm that genuinely practices collaborative matrimonial law and does not litigate, or a construction company with fair prices that shows up on schedule and cleans up after itself.

There are people doing all of these. They operate differently from the first two business owners I mentioned. They mean to change the world they live in for the better. They mean to dominate in their marketplace, whether it's the whole world or their own town. And when they need resources, they figure out how to get them.

Plan C

Any of these games is vastly different from your corporate career. If you are among the Formerly Corporate™, you can choose which one to play. And if you started in one game, there's nothing to stop you from moving to another. Just remember that we keep score by selling something at a profit.

Chapter 6
Entrepreneur Land
Can Be Lonely If You Let It

One of the things people often devalue in their transition is how important the social structure of their workplace was.

Even looking for the coffee pot on a new job can remind you that you're in unfamiliar territory. Now that you're permanently "out of the office," where's the coffee pot? Not the one in your kitchen, but the one where you find your colleagues, catch up on last night's game and speculate on the latest things the management is up to.

It was not only the camaraderie, but knowing the pecking order, where you fit in and who the "go-to" people were, that contributed to a sense of security that meant so much.

The loss of that security is profound, but it can take a while for it to sink in. When it does, often after Plan B loses its momentum, ask yourself what you need to do about this as you move to Plan C. Build a network? Find a coffee shop? Invite people to meet with you?

The spotlight won't shine on you without effort

We touched on this earlier, but it bears elaboration. It goes back to a skewed perception of your own impact—if you don't think highly of yourself, you will not be successful in business. However, it's unlikely that you are such a star that the spotlight will turn naturally to you.

Celebrities have teams to get the lights bright and focused on them. They have agents and managers and publicists. They have photographers and make-up artists and stylists. They get on TV and YouTube and Twitter and *The New York Times*. They don't do it by themselves.

One of the first tasks after being set adrift is to find your bearings. Where are you, and how will you figure it out? In business, it's not so easy to find out who can really help. Who should we listen to?

Don't listen only to yourself

Now I don't mean you shouldn't trust your instincts or do your own analysis or make the final decisions for your own business. I mean listening to

79

yourself as the dictator, the "my way or the highway" kind of guy, or the isolated, behind the screen, "I don't need people" (what about customers?) techie, or the "I just want to help people" alternative health or life coach stereotype.

If you stay isolated, you'll be limited to your own ideas, experience and perspective. And when you realize that, you'll also recognize the need to hire, manage, delegate, train, coach and tolerate other people so they can provide their unique skills and business view to your enterprise.

Unless you want to do everything yourself forever (in which case you'll never be the Conquering Entrepreneur, or even a very successful sole practitioner), you need other people's ideas. But whose?

Don't listen too much to people too much like you

Now that may seem odd coming from me, since peer-advisory or mastermind groups are the heart of my business practice. Notice I didn't say, "*don't listen to people like yourself.*" Peers at a similar stage of business to yours, or in a similar business sector, can be invaluable. If you are not in some kind of peer-advisory or mastermind group, you are well advised to get yourself into one.

A peer group I was in myself for a while had a sales manager, an attorney, an award-winning salesperson, a marketing expert, an IT generalist, several networking experts and me—the engineer. Weird bunch, huh? I never would have seen business through the lenses they did.

Look for people who have different businesses, business models, personalities, leadership styles from yours. Your options will expand, and therefore your decisions will be better informed. And quite different from what you would come up with on your own.

The person who said, condescendingly, "Why in the world would I want to be in a group with a personal chef?" shut right up when I replied, "Do you think her twenty years in direct marketing could be of any benefit to you?"

In addition, the Plan C entrepreneur seeks expert help from business owners a step or two beyond his or her current stage of business. I always describe the transitions between one stage of a business and another—say, from working at home to getting an office, or from running everything yourself to hiring a project manager or chief operating officer—as pinch points. Because they hurt.

When you have someone to talk to who has been through that transition, you can save a lot of boneheaded moves and the resultant headaches. Hiring (and firing) employees is as much art as business, and building your skills just in that one arena can be accelerated by talking to others ahead of you.

Now I've had business owners say to me, somewhat selfishly, "I don't want to be the most experienced person in the mastermind group. I want to learn from those ahead of me." To that I have to ask, "Well, someone has to be the least experienced, and someone has to be the most experienced, right? What makes you think someone behind you, so to speak, doesn't have something to teach you?"

So invest in yourself and your business, in terms of money, time and energy, to learn from others, **before** you've wasted that much money, time and energy, or more, trying to do it all yourself.

In a mastermind group in early 2009, when all were worried about their 401(k)s and where their next business credit line would come from, a twenty-year veteran of her own marketing business declared, to enthusiastic agreement, "I'd rather invest in myself right now than in any bank or cooked-up financial instrument!"

Wise advice.

I had those "go-to" people right here!

At least you knew in your corporate world who the "go-to" people were. In your new world, and in the new game, you don't necessarily know where they are or whom to trust.

You might have tried in your Plan B phase the do-it-all-myself approach. You've stopped that, right? However, with your Conquering Entrepreneur lenses clean, you see that you need new reliability partners. You are ready to find, use and celebrate the resources you really need to make Plan C work. Congratulate yourself on a smart business decision as well as getting some monkeys off your back.

Here are just a few areas where you probably need help:

- Marketing strategy and execution
- PR and advertising
- Fund-raising
- Copywriting
- Bookkeeping and accounting
- Web design and maintenance
- Office assistance, virtual or in-house

Unless you are an expert yourself in one of those fields, find some experts and let them help you. Talk to marketing experts—they can give you some direction and a plan. Even if you execute it yourself, at least you're not floundering in the sea of possibilities. Engage a bookkeeper and an accountant—before tax filing time! Find a mom who wants to work part-time, or a virtual assistant. Actually, those are often the same, and can do many of the functions mentioned.

Don't get lost among self-proclaimed experts

This trap can be seductive and hard to escape. It's the information marketing age. Half the world and their cousins seem to be blogging, doing teleseminars and webinars and videos, vying for your attention with the latest and greatest tips, tools, tricks to solve whatever problem they think you have.

I have spent a lot of my own time and quite a few

dollars to find people who could teach and guide me, at the time and with the focus that I need. (Truthfully, I often waited too long.) Even the ones who weren't "right" led me eventually to ones who turned out to be exactly what I needed. Just be cautious of people who try to fit you into their solution, like you are one of Cinderella's stepsisters. Hold out for help that fits your situation.

So here's where the Plan C attitude kicks in. You used to have resources at your fingertips. Now you don't. So look for trustworthy people and get yourself some help.

Don't know how to find the experts? We talked a lot earlier about your budding network. Here's one place those people come in very handy. Ask *them*.

If that gives you pause, you're probably ready for another shift in your mindset. There's another misconception many people have, especially if, within your corporate setting, the tacit agreement was to stick to your knitting and solve your own problems.

You don't want to bother your connections!

What are connections for, anyway? Any connection—former boss, former colleague, school pal, kid's soccer coach, even the "out-of-reach" people a level or two above you in that old hierarchy—are probably willing to hear a bit about what you are doing or planning in your new Entrepreneur Land. They will probably be interested, even excited for you, and maybe a teeny bit envious.

Yet you might hesitate to call on the people who know you best and could help the most—it's risky to put yourself out there to people you know. They might think you are overreaching, or bound to fail, or they just don't have time at the moment for you. And also, former colleagues might be the ones who "let you go." Eeewwww.

You'd rather find all new people and start from scratch! That is short-sighted. You need both perspectives.

You have more leverage and power than you think

This is very important. Why do I say that? Several reasons:

First, with today's tools such as LinkedIn, Facebook, YouTube and all the other upstarts starting up in that space, it is easier than ever to reconnect with people you used to know.

Those tools are mainstream now. New business ideas, useful tips and how-to's, job postings and just ways to ask a question or start a conversation—all are a part of normal business discourse. Find a few groups that interest you, participate in the discussions, ask and answer some questions. You'll establish or reestablish yourself as a contributing member of the business community, and people who know you will be curious to see what you're up to.

You reappear in their world as an interesting, can-do, "what's she up to now?" contact. Now leverage that!

Second, it is true that you need to meet new people. But not just by finding them individually, or cold calling, or mass emailing, although all of those techniques work. They are just minded numbing and/or inefficient.

Learn to network—really network, not just sling around business cards. Join a networking group, such as BNI. Join your local business association—even if your business is not geographically limited. Find out where your prospective clients hang out and go there.

If you sell online or through webinars and such, find people with complementary products or services and co-market to each other's lists. This last is a huge opportunity that many small business people overlook—your list of prospects and clients is the most valuable asset your company owns, and the online community is willing to help build each other's lists under mutually beneficial circumstances.

This is not a how-to network book—there are excellent books in the reference section. Please read them, but remember that networking is a verb—it's an action to take, repeatedly, until you get to be stellar at it, and learn to capitalize your connections.

And third, why did I say you have more power than you think? Because with strong connections, you can become a master of leverage. Who you know, who they know, who they know—drill down until you find the right resource for yourself or the people you are trying to serve—your customers.

As you build your own resources, you can exercise

your leverage. You can access, or help others to access, new markets. You can find help with any operation your business needs, or that another contact needs. You will know bankers and attorneys and financial planners and insurance agents who you come to trust. You can get anything done—from estate planning to vacation planning. Maybe you barter, maybe you refer, maybe you hire. Maybe you become a job creator. Now that would be leverage!

Patience is a virtue

Here will be your biggest challenge in this area: You may be quite impatient with this process. The Formerly Corporate™ are used to having all the resources they need. Oh, I know they complained that they needed a bigger budget or more people or better equipment, but in general the resources were there. Of course, you used to be someone else's resource, and it's no fun being left behind to do three people's work, either. Been there, done that.

In this new game, you have to drill for resources in a different way, but drill you must. To make a real impact with your own Plan C, marshal your connections and colleagues and friends and acquaintances. Let people know what you are looking for.

And pay it forward—better advice was never put in so few words.

Remember: Plan A was your first career, and Plan B was the first business you started or the first

Lorette Pruden

business model you tried. Plan C is what you create now with all that you've learned and digested.

The Conquering Entrepreneur plays the Plan C game for real—for real money, for real influence, for real impact. Are you ready? You may have to get out of your own way first.

SECTION THREE

The Conquering
Entrepreneur Stumbles

Focus. Accountability. Urgency

Chapter 7
Your Own Worst Enemy

We have met the enemy and he is us.
Walt Kelly

In the words of many exasperated compatriots and family members, whether in business or at home, the Formerly Corporate™ have a major challenge in their transition: **Get over yourself.**

Whether you were a C-suite executive, or an employee whose worth and skill were undervalued, you will need to resolve (mostly for yourself) the question:

Don't they know who I used to be?

The short answer is no. Even if they do know, they don't care.

Now I'm not trying to curb your enthusiasm. You'll need it! But the Plan B entrepreneur, fresh out of the corporate box, falls into two categories:

1. *Enamored of the bright-and-shiny Former Self:*

Here I come, the new business owner, eager, full of confidence, radiating my former glory. Business—customers, clients—will beat a path to my door!

2: *Shedding the light-under-a-bushel Former Self:*

They never appreciated me anyway. I'm going to reinvent myself and do what I always wanted to do. Business—customers, clients—will beat a path to my door!

Both of these starting points can lead to success in the new game of your own business. But I'm here to tell you, and so could many others ahead of you in the journey:

That path people are supposed to beat to your door can be mighty faint! You will have to go to the marketplace, find and fill a vacuum, and get visible and stay visible.

Illuminating that path so people will come to you becomes more challenging every day:

Websites, blogs, ezines, articles, PR, interviews, Facebook, LinkedIn, Twitter, whatever will be next—and that's just the online part. There's networking, developing face-to-face relationships, cultivating referrals (that's giving as well as hoping for), becoming known in your physical community, sponsoring the ball team.

Whether you picture yourself as the beacon or the bushel, your willingness to embrace your present situation—accept what's working and what needs to change—will be key to the next phase of your success.

Here are some examples:

You may be pretty good at what you do—it's just that you don't do marketing or sales. Or worse: You may believe that "marketing" is something that creeps do to manipulate you, and that "sales," as a profession, is smarmy and manipulative, and, quite frankly, beneath you.

At best, you may think marketing and sales are necessary, just not what you are good at. The shortest path to the cash for you will be to get better at it.

Someone knows how, and is willing to teach you. Sign up for sales training, take a marketing course, spring for a marketing plan done by/with a professional, hire a virtual assistant with Internet marketing skills.

Or you may realize that public speaking is a good business development tool. It's not too hard to find people to speak to—local networking groups, your trade association local chapters, Chambers of Commerce are always looking for speakers. And you might be a pretty good speaker.

But if you choose this path, you need to become a really good speaker. Even if you don't dream of the spotlight and the keynote speech, every encounter is an opportunity to speak to your potential clients. The shorter the speech, the harder it is. How good is your elevator speech? Your two-minute elaboration. What if someone would listen to you for five minutes? Or to a whole sales presentation? Again, this is a learnable skill, not just an innate talent.

Here's a bit of my own story: I knew public

speaking would be good for my business, and I was not shy about it. My father was a minister and my mother a teacher, so fear of public speaking was not in my genes. I could tell a pretty good story, people said, so I looked for opportunities to speak early in the life of my Plan B business.

Then I ran into people from the National Speakers Association. They got paid to speak. Well, I asked, how do you do THAT?

Drawn into the world of professional speaking, I learned, first, how much I didn't know. Then I learned where I could improve the most in the shortest time. I took workshops in stage presence (you wouldn't believe what it takes to enter a room or onto a stage with just the right amount of swagger—the bigger the room, the more swagger. That was really hard for me.) I learned how to preserve my voice when speaking all day long. I learned to craft a speech in chunks so I could remember it. And I learned how to preserve the core message when the person ahead of me hogged my time.

I even took an improvisational acting course, which, believe me, has come in handy in some bizarre circumstances. What do you do with a heckler? Or an in-your-face competitor? Or when someone complains that your price is outrageous? You'd better be ready to do some fancy dancin'!

Along the way, I qualified for membership in the National Speakers Association, and served our state chapter on the Board and then as chapter president. It's been an investment of my time, budget and energy that continues to pay off, in business opportunities, speaking and consulting fees, new friends and lots of fun.

But even if you just want to be more comfortable speaking, you can improve a lot. Take a public speaking course, spend some time with Toastmasters International or find a private speech coach to help you with a major presentation. It will help you get yourself over, as well as get over yourself.

Suppose you are already a whiz at marketing and sales and are a silver-tongued charmer?

I would bet then that you're not so good at creating systems for your business, at doing the harder things consistently and with excellence, so your customers have a consistently excellent experience with your company

Then it's time to polish that up. Not just your public persona but also your back office operations.

Your first website may have been put up by your teenager. Mine was. Then I got invited to speak at University of Pennsylvania Wharton School of Business. Uh-oh. That "business card website" was not going to impress those folks! I spent 18 hours building myself a new one. It worked for the time being, but I am not a website designer, SEO optimizer or graphic artist.

And that field evolves so quickly that the time for a new website seems to come right on the heels of the last one you put up. In today's world, you may need multiple websites, sales pages, auto-responder items and more. Plus a Facebook page, and a LinkedIn presence and a social marketing strategy...

Eventually, you'll see the wisdom of getting professional help.

Or how do you bill your clients? Haphazardly? I'm sorry to say, some people do. Then they wonder why the clients pay haphazardly. Here are a few ways to fix this problem:

Use written agreements so payment terms are clear. Simple is fine for smaller deals. Get a lawyer to write you a general agreement for larger projects.

Find a part-time bookkeeper. Get set up right. Keep up with your billing. Invoice regularly. Follow up promptly. You are only asking for what they agreed to pay you. There's no need to feel embarrassed or to be overly aggressive.

If you behave like a "real business," people will respond accordingly. And you might not have to hire a bill-collection service.

I remember one client who took a different tack here. He had had a long career in a family-run retail business. He was used to ringing out the register, and tallying the take. His work was not over until the day's receipts were entered and the books balanced. He was good at bookkeeping.

Rather than pay for a bookkeeper, it was a better use of his resources to hire a coach and get focused on targeting prospects, and following up with them. Or finding other ways to generate revenues. Or saving operating costs. So he would have something in the cash register to tally.

Get help with whatever your business needs that

you don't have the skills for. Step out of the spotlight for a while, and become a student of the skills that will make your Plan C business work.

Notice I didn't say "learn the skills" but "become a student of them." Mastery is a long-term process, perhaps a lifelong process. If you are willing to expand your own self-image from "I got it" to "I'm getting it," you will find your business more interesting and more profitable.

Rather than staying stuck with the (admittedly amazing) skills you brought with you into business, you will look back in a little while at what you have learned, applied and created for Plan C, and marvel.

Another way to be your own worst enemy:

Let yourself off the hook.

If you're the boss, even of just yourself, who else knows what you said you would do that you haven't done? So many other things came up. It's just your internal dialogue anyway. You're only deceiving—who?

Focus. Accountability. Urgency.

These are the three blocks that my Formerly Corporate™ clients have told me they stumble on the most.

Focus: There are just so many more things that need the business owner's attention in Entrepreneur Land than in your corporate position. The stack of hats on your head threatens to topple at every moment. The sheer volume of decisions to make can be overwhelming.

And the bright and shiny syndrome kicks in here as well. Now it's about your new idea, or a new product or target market—if you just run and CATCH THAT, problems solved!

Which problem? Often, it's the boredom and lack of focus, the reluctance to settle down and do the WORK of your current business that you're looking for a way out of. Finishing something – a project, a book, a website—seems less attractive than starting something. Friends, the solution lies on the other side of the work—the finished product, the sales campaign, the article written, the clients serviced.

(Productivity is part of the issue here, because you need systems and helpers to get everything done.)

Continually, the Conquering Entrepreneur re-focuses.

- On the clear picture you drew of why you are in business anyway, who you are trying to serve, how you will help them and what you need to do to serve that market.
- On the highest priority accomplishments.
- On the highest and best use of your time.

If you take a detour, make it a conscious decision. It's OK to change tacks. The journey to a successful Plan C business will not go in a straight line. In fact, it will become necessary at some point to recalculate the best course forward. But don't let it be because you lost focus on the direction you are heading.

Accountability: "I need some accountability for myself," said Jonathan, who stepped in to help out, and perhaps take over, a family business. "The culture around here has always been to do everything, to step in and do the $10 an hour job if no one is in place to do it. The idea of choosing to do the $400 job instead doesn't really occur to the others." The reason Jonathan was talking to an accountability coach was that, even realizing what he'd just said, he knew the temptation to drift off his focus was too high to risk it alone.

I've often said I don't think you can sell "accountability" but some people see their need, want to be held to account and are willing to pay for it. Why? Because they know the temptation to swerve, or drift, to a less demanding task is eternal. They want someone to ask:

"Have you worked on that long-term project this week? What about that important stretch goal to create a new division, or to develop a new market segment? Or the research you needed to do about labor laws for your first hire, or first fire? What have you done about those?"

Urgency: Remember in the last chapter I said patience is a virtue. True, and so is urgency. To begin. To finish.

> *He has half the deed done*
> *who has made a beginning.*
>
> *Horace*

It's almost done. All I have left is to finish it up.
a friend of my brother's

Between the beginning and the finishing, one of the most effective things a business owner can do is to get the ball into someone else's court—someone who will be responsible for the next move.

- Finish the wireframe for your new website, and SEND IT to the web designer.
- Scan your receipts daily or weekly and SEND THEM to the bookkeeper.
- Write a series of blog posts or Twitter feeds and SCHEDULE THEM, so a software program sends them out for you.

With those off your desk, and others working on your behalf, you can go on to longer term projects that only you can do.

- Design your next product. Get a prototype made and show it to a few people. THEN digest the feedback you get.
- Figure out where your ideal customer might be found. Ask around. THEN go meet them.
- Outline your book. Write your first draft of your next program or article. Send it to someone else for their reaction. THEN write the next draft.

It's very hard to stay focused on activities that the CEO (that's you) should do, and not get drawn off into supporting roles and tasks that your employees, your Starburst Business™ partners, or some temporary helpers are best suited for.

Here's where the focus, accountability and urgency merge, and where having someone to refocus you, ask hard questions and kick your behind makes you better as a businessperson:

"We talked about where you see this business in the next year, or three. All those new website sketches are fine. But what about last week's or last month's or last quarter's targets? Did you hit them? And you didn't really spend two hours reworking the schedule, did you? Isn't that Chris's job?"

Focus is easily lost. Accountability is hard won. Urgency is often avoided.

Focus. Accountability. Now.

Open up your thinking. Unless, or even if, you led your corporation and had to do big-picture thinking on a regular basis, you may have overdeveloped the mode of logical, linear thinking.

When the path forward and the ways to measure progress have been set, it's not so hard to march along that path and accomplish a lot—this many sales, these new product tweaks, that much code written. Systematic thinking, project planning and management, and enterprise relationship software pull it all together and present left brain-driven solutions and accomplishments.

But when you have to create the destination for

yourself, and figure out how to get there, and how to know where you are on the journey, linear thinking is often not the best approach.

Recent research on human cognition suggests that leaders would do better to use associative thinking *to spot, act on, and legitimize distant opportunities.*

This way of thinking suggests that a crucial component of strategic leadership is the mental capacity to spot opportunities that are invisible to rivals and to manage other relevant parties' perceptions to get them on board. [7]

The more associative your thinking can be in the strategic realm of your business, the more likely you are to come up with something new, or a different way to do things, or think of unlikely people who could help you. Try thinking in pictures before you put words and outlines and process maps to the task. Draw. Ok, sketch. All right, doodle.

Remember that improvisational acting class? You're not trying to become a fine artist or a Shakespearean actor. You're trying to jog your brain into a new outlook. Go ahead. You don't have to justify your thought processes to the "boss" any more. Remember you're the boss. Wake up. Open up. Wise up.

Then you can move up.

---

[7] Giovanni Gavetti, Harvard Business Review
http://hbr.org/2011/07/the-new-psychology-of-strategic-leadership/ar/1

SECTION FOUR

Solutions: All Hail the Conquering Entrepreneur

How to create money out of thin air

Chapter 8
How to Recognize
That Conquering Entrepreneur

Who is the Conquering Entrepreneur? What does she, the CE as well as the CEO, look like?

From personal experience and from observing hundreds of people going through this mindset shift, I've come to believe that the successful transition from corporate employee to Conquering Entrepreneur involves three characteristics:

- Embracing ambiguity
- Accepting volatility
- Creating money out of thin air

Let me elaborate.

Lorette Pruden

The Conquering Entrepreneur
embraces ambiguity

Acceptance is key here. The Conquering Entrepreneur accepts that he can't know it all, can't have it
all and can't do it all. Of course, "it" must be known,
obtained or completed for the enterprise to become
successful. So accepting, even joyfully seeking, help
from others is critical. The who, the where do I find
them, the how do I get them to do it as well as I do—
those questions are part of embracing ambiguity.
There's no definite right answer to them.

The Conquering Entrepreneur is willing to set off
without a roadmap. It's best to have a destination in
mind, but even so, the CE understands that she
cannot know exactly how things will go. She can only
plot a course, follow it and make adjustments along
the way. She will encounter people who can see
further than she can. They may be ahead on the path
or just on a higher path altogether. The CE tries to see
through his or her binoculars, or perhaps his or her
telescope. Her business vision changes as she gets
deeper into the realities of her chosen business. It may
just clear up. It will probably grow bigger. Isn't that
exciting!

The Conquering Entrepreneur's underlying
attitude becomes, "Isn't this a great life?" I've yet to
find someone committed to the entrepreneurial life
who would be happy going back to a corporate job.
Even with the challenges (remember recreating your
own self-image, focusing and re-focusing seeking

106

accountability, risking the house, expanding your thinking), the CE gets up in the morning and thinks: "Another great day!" If it's raining, it's a great day to get down to business on a redesign of something. If it's sunny, it might be a great day to spend time with clients and prospects. If's it's a "meh" day, it's still a great time to pick a smaller project and knock it off the list.

Isn't this a great life?

The Conquering Entrepreneur accepts volatility

The larger economy seems indecipherable. The safety net is no longer there. Home equity and maybe retirement savings have been invested in the business and/or evaporated. The banks won't lend money.

Most entrepreneurs will risk almost everything for the freedom to create, to engage, to climb the barriers, to plot their own course. The Conquering Entrepreneur seizes the chance and Plan B becomes Plan C.

Though most small business owners are control freaks, the Conquering Entrepreneur sees a bigger picture. Market forces do swing wildly. Target markets are elusive. But the Conquering Entrepreneur realizes it has ever been thus. It's OK.

These last few years have been uncharted territory. Yet more and more people start businesses, and some of them become successful. Of the many life lessons in the Berenstain Bears books, I remember best the approach from *The Big Road Race*: "Over, under and around and through, went Orange, Yellow, Green and Blue."

The Conquering Entrepreneur will figure something out, and try it. And if it looks like it's working, he'll build systems and hire assistants to keep the money coming in, so he can stay free to show the next characteristic.

The Conquering Entrepreneur creates money out of thin air

That's what a business does. Goods or services are offered to a buyer in exchange for money.

Where did the goods or services come from? The Conquering Entrepreneur makes them. Maybe he planted the seeds and harvested the crops, or drilled for natural resources, or used his own creativity and wrote a book. And there was support from others along the way: Maybe he took some courses at the local Small Business Development Center, a federal government program, or the state department of labor. Maybe he hired a business coach, or joined a mastermind group.

But none of these products would have made it to the marketplace without the application of knowledge, ingenuity, hard work and discipline. People who don't have your particular knowledge, ingenuity, hard work and discipline are willing to pay money for yours. And vice versa.

At first, the entrepreneur operates without the security of a paycheck. But job security is not so secure anymore, anyway. No one owes you a living.

Those goods and services must be produced and delivered. Those sales must be sought and won. The Conquering Entrepreneur figures out how to do that and does it consistently. Money materializes from the thin air of imagination, is refined through the crucible of hard work and deposits itself into the CE's bank account. Oh, I know it's all electrons now, no more gold. Still, how cool is that?

Ambiguity. Volatility. Creativity.

The Conquering Entrepreneur.

Chapter 9
What's Next? Your Own Plan C

One of those three traits—embracing ambiguity, accepting volatility and creating money out of thin air—will be more comfortable for you than the others. And one will probably seem very difficult. That means that working with a strength and vanquishing a fear greatly increase your odds of success. Let's see if we can tease out where you fall on the spectrum.

How to recognize yourself as a Conquering Entrepreneur

First of all, there are some commonly held ideas out there that apply to some businesses but may not apply to yours.

Which of these are true or false for the business you want to create?

Ten *True/False/It Depends* Statements
for the Conquering Entrepreneur

_____ A business is very difficult to start.

_____ It will be three years before a new business becomes profitable.

_____ The best advice comes from those in my type of business.

_____ It's my business—and my schedule is my own.

_____ I need to know how to do everything myself, even if I hire someone else to do it.

_____ What goes around, comes around.

_____ My best first hire is someone like me.

_____ People will help, even if I can't pay.

_____ I seek out and pay for professional advice.

_____ Structuring my time and space pays off.

Every person will answer these questions differently. There is no one right or wrong answer. Business is an art, not a science, and your skill set, your experience, your stage of business and your temperament will influence how you answer them.

111

Look over the answers to your questions, particularly those that you answered with "it depends," or that you know you would have answered differently at an earlier stage of your business, and think about this:

What circumstances or lessons learned caused you to change your approach?

How did you embrace ambiguity, accept volatility and/or create money out of thin air?

On the next few pages are some statements to help you explore those questions at a deeper level. As you reflect on and work with these ideas, your confidence and competence as a CE will grow. Write down your answers and save them to look at in six months or a year. You may be surprised at how your answers will change.

Here are statements that you might take more than one way. Which ones illustrate a positive ambiguity for you? Where can you see that the other side of the statement could also be true for you? Write a few words (it's ok, it's your book!) about those. Or go to www.formerlycorporate.com/Ch9—questions to save your answers to your computer.

Embracing Ambiguity:

I have to have a recognizable brand to be successful.

_____

_____

_____

_____

_____

_____

_____

_____

_____

_____

_____

_____

My former colleagues are eager to hire me.

_____

_____

_____

_____

_____

_____

_____

_____

_____

Asking for help is a sign of weakness.

_____

_____

_____

_____

_____

_____

_____

_____

_____

Other people have expertise I don't.

_____

_____

_____

_____

_____

_____

_____

_____

_____

There's no time to take time off. I need to stay focused and get the job done.

_____

_____

_____

_____

_____

_____

_____

_____

_____

You have to get away to get ahead.

_____

_____

_____

_____

_____

_____

_____

_____

_____

There's no one who fits my job criteria.

_____

_____

_____

_____

_____

_____

_____

_____

_____

I could create a job for this good person.

_____

_____

_____

_____

_____

_____

_____

_____

_____

Accepting volatility:
If my profits are not growing consistently, I'm in the wrong business.

_____

_____

_____

_____

_____

_____

_____

_____

_____

Lorette Pruden

Help can be had without hiring full-time but they may not be there when I really need them.

_____

_____

_____

_____

_____

_____

_____

_____

People are too hard to manage. Some people, some of the time.

_____

_____

_____

_____

_____

_____

_____

_____

There's only so much (and it's very little) control I have over the larger economy.

_____

_____

_____

_____

_____

_____

_____

_____

_____

Government rules and regulations change too frequently or not often enough.

_____

_____

_____

_____

_____

_____

_____

_____

Lorette Pruden

The market and how I approach it is a moving target.

_____

_____

_____

_____

_____

_____

_____

_____

I know a lot but have to learn more, starting with "customers come and go".

_____

_____

_____

_____

_____

_____

_____

_____

_____

Creating money out of thin air. That's what a business does.

_____

_____

_____

_____

_____

_____

_____

_____

I succeed by my own initiative and hard work.

_____

_____

_____

_____

_____

_____

_____

_____

_____

A Starburst Business™ organization makes sense for me.

_____

_____

_____

_____

_____

_____

_____

_____

I need some other business owners to talk to.

_____

_____

_____

_____

_____

_____

_____

_____

_____

_____

Choosing the right complementary business and business owner is key to mutual success.

_____

_____

_____

_____

_____

_____

_____

_____

I provide professional services myself, so I am willing to pay for the services of other professionals.

_____

_____

_____

_____

_____

_____

_____

_____

123

If you build it, they will come—if you invite them.

As you consider what you have learned so far, and what changes you've already made, you will probably decide to direct your business differently.

Your own Plan C

OK, you've identified the game. You've learned some of the rules. You see where you can get in your own way. You are still Formerly Corporate™, but that's now an advantage to build on, not a cliff to jump off of. As the fog clears from the mirror, you see the conquering hero's reflection—and he is YOU.

You are ready to refine your game plan to meet the circumstances, and you are becoming, more and more, a Conquering Entrepreneur. So let's get practical. First, on the next few pages, take an inventory:

Your best talents and skills from your Plan A corporate career.

_____

_____

_____

_____

_____

_____

_____

_____

The highest impact learning you took from Plan B— what you didn't know then but know now.

_____

_____

_____

_____

_____

_____

_____

_____

What you would like your business to be, do and have at its pinnacle. Some would call this your vision.

_____

_____

_____

_____

_____

_____

_____

_____

_____

What you would like your business to be, do and have over the next two years?

_____

_____

_____

_____

_____

_____

_____

Information, introspection, into action

With this book, you have had a chance to get some information and to do some introspection. Now it is time to put it into action for you!

Look over the answers you have written and the lists you have made and combine these into your very own Plan C. It's OK if it's not perfect yet. When I began to talk about the concept for this book, someone said to me, "I'm on Plan Q already...is that a problem?" To my mind, keep learning, keep growing, keep tweaking, keep improving. The designers of Excel realized that you might need more than 26 columns. If you reach Z, you can continue with AA.

But for now, concentrate on Plan C. Welcome to Entrepreneur Land!

Resources

Books

Business by Referral, Ivan R. Misner and Robert Davis, Bard Press, 1997, 2006

Endless Referrals, Bob Burg, McGraw-Hill, 1999

The E-Myth, The E-Myth Revisited, E-Myth Mastery, Michael Gerber, Harper-Collins, 1990, 1995, 2007

The Great Road Race, Stan and Jan Berenstain, Random House, 1987.

Websites

Entrepreneurs University, a non-profit educational institution for entrepreneurial CEOs, entreuniv.org

Ewing Marion Kauffman Foundation, kauffman.org

GUST.com, Matching angel investors & entrepreneurs

National Speakers Association, www.nsaspeakers.org

United States Small Business Association, www.sba.gov, www.SBDC.org, www.SCORE.org

The Center for Association Leadership, www.asaecenter.org

Weddles Directory of Associations, www.Weddles.com/associations

State Economic Development Departments
Most states have an economic development department. Check online at your state's website for more information.

www.njeda.gov. Also each township has an Economic Business Development Commission.

Non-profit economic development organizations, www.UCEDC.com

Regional Business Assistance Corporation, www.RBACloan.com

For freelance assistance with many office, productivity and marketing needs:

www.o-Desk.com, www.Fiverr.com

International Virtual Assistants Association. www.ivaa.org

National Association of Professional Organizers, NAPO.org

About the Author

Working at the intersection of business and people processes, Lorette Pruden, PhD, has helped hundreds of small business owners, start-up entrepreneurs, sales professionals and community leaders grow their businesses and manage that growth. Her clients say she directly impacts their bottom line, in time, energy and money. Many of those clients have left the corporate world to start and run businesses of their own.

Lorette is a Princeton chemical engineer-turned-entrepreneur. Formerly with Mobil, in business for herself since 2000, Lorette speaks, consults and writes on the transition from working for others to building a successful business. With Formerly Corporate™, she lays out the path for the erstwhile employee to become a successful business owner.

Lorette lives, works, and when not inciting the Formerly Corporate™, manages her local farmers market in central New Jersey.

www.ingramcontent.com/pod-product-compliance
Lightning Source LLC
Chambersburg PA
CBHW071149200326
41519CB00018B/5168